NATIONAL GEOGRAPHIC
School Publishing

Plantas

Mary Garcia

PICTURE CREDITS

Illustrations by Karen Ahlschlager (4–5, 14–15).
Cover, 8 (left), 10 (left), 11 (right), 10 (right), 16 (above left
& above right), Getty Images; 2, 6 (all), 7 (all), 9 (inset), 11 (above right), 12 (above right
& below right), 13, 16 (center left & center right), APL/Corbis; 9 (left), Zefa Images.

Produced through the worldwide resources of the National Geographic Society, John M. Fahey,
Jr., President and Chief Executive Officer; Gilbert M. Grosvenor, Chairman of the Board.

PREPARED BY NATIONAL GEOGRAPHIC SCHOOL PUBLISHING

Ericka Markman, Senior Vice President and President Children's Books and Education
Publishing Group; Steve Mico, Senior Vice President and Publisher; Marianne Hiland,
Editorial Director; Lynnette Brent, Executive Editor; Michael Murphy and Barbara Wood,
Senior Editors; Bea Jackson, Design Director; David Dumo, Art Director; Margaret
Sidlowsky, Illustrations Director; Matt Wascavage, Manager of Publishing Services;
Sean Philpotts, Production Manager.

SPANISH LANGUAGE VERSION PREPARED BY
NATIONAL GEOGRAPHIC SCHOOL PUBLISHING GROUP

Sheron Long, CEO; Sam Gesumaria, President; Fran Downey, Vice President and Publisher;
Margaret Sidlosky, Director of Design and Illustrations; Paul Osborn, Senior Editor; Sean
Philpotts, Project Manager; Lisa Pergolizzi, Production Manager.

MANUFACTURING AND QUALITY MANAGEMENT

Christopher A. Liedel, Chief Financial Officer; George Bounelis, Vice President;
Clifton M. Brown III, Director.

BOOK DEVELOPMENT

Ibis for Kids Australia Pty Limited

SPANISH LANGUAGE TRANSLATION

Tatiana Acosta/Guillermo Gutiérrez

SPANISH LANGUAGE BOOK DEVELOPMENT

Navta Associates, Inc.

Published by the National Geographic Society
Washington, D.C. 20036-4688

ISBN: 978-0-7362-3827-4

Printed in Mexico

Print Number: 03   Print Year: 2023

Contenido

flor

arbusto

árbol frutal

hoja

¿Qué plantas ven?
¿Qué partes tienen?

árbol frutal

semillas de girasol

plantas de tomate

plantas de lechuga

plantas de fresa

Hojas

La mayoría de las plantas tienen hojas.

Estos árboles tienen hojas.

Estos nenúfares tienen hojas.

Estas plantas tienen hojas.

Flores

Muchas plantas tienen flores.

Este arbusto tiene flores.

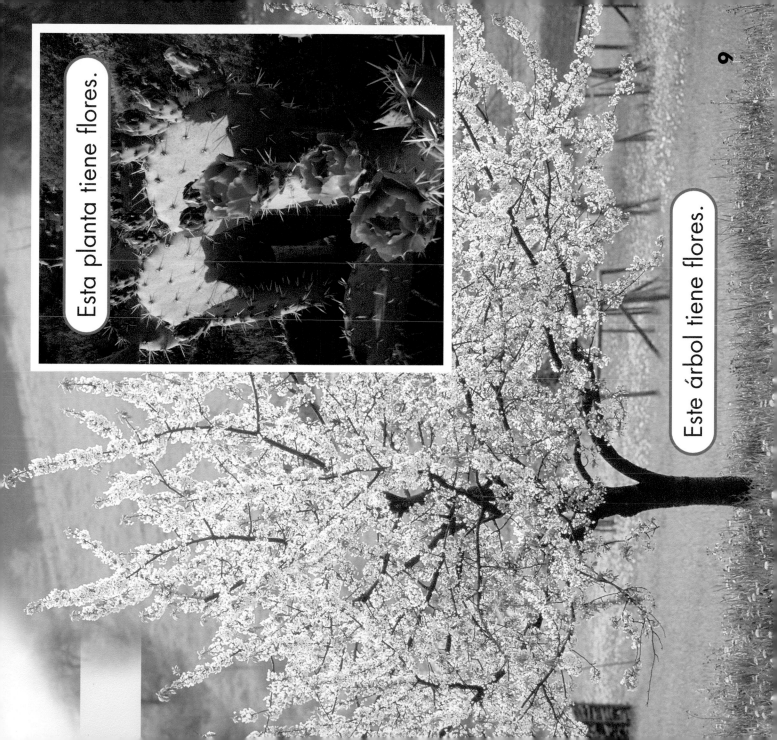

Esta planta tiene flores.

Este árbol tiene flores.

Frutos

Algunas plantas tienen frutos.

Este árbol tiene frutos.

Esta vid tiene frutos.

Este arbusto tiene frutos.

Esta planta tiene frutos.

Crecer y cambiar

Todas las plantas crecen y cambian. La mayoría de las plantas salen de semillas.

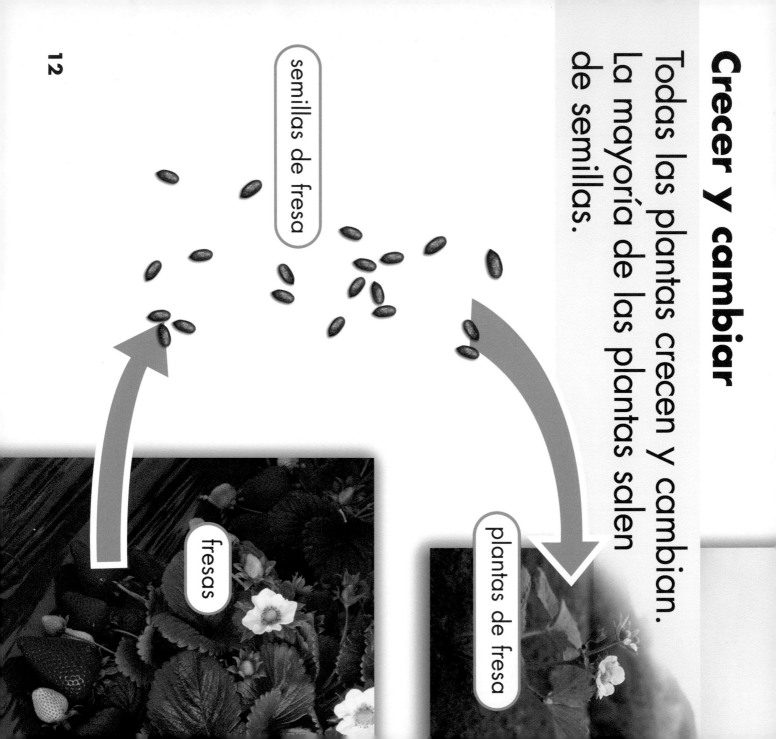

semillas de fresa

plantas de fresa

fresas

flores de la fresa

Usar lo que aprendieron

manzano

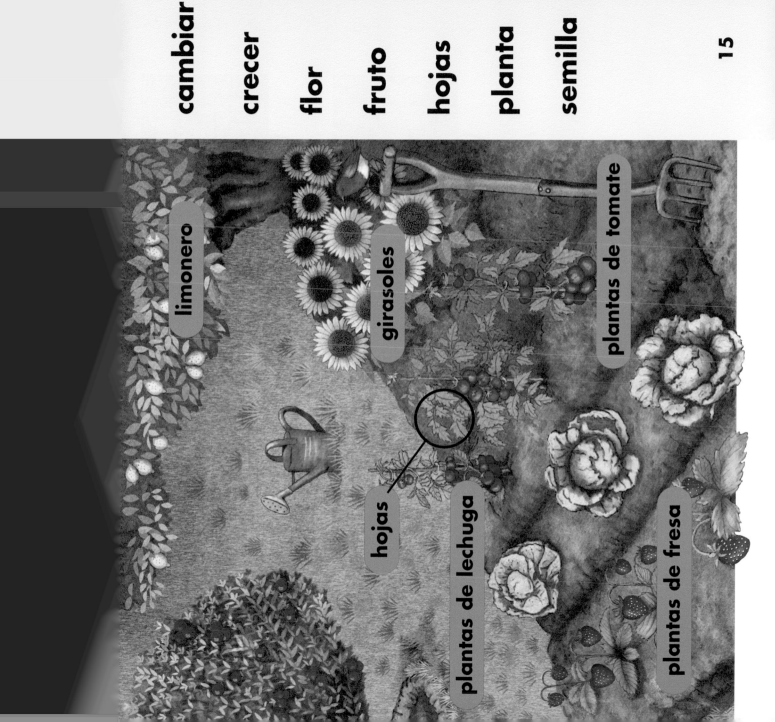

cambiar

crecer

flor

fruto

hojas

planta

semilla

limonero

girasoles

plantas de tomate

hojas

plantas de lechuga

plantas de fresa

Glosario ilustrado

hojas

flores

semillas

plantas

frutos